a forever kind of dream

ifeanyi ogbo

bobtimystic
BOOKS

A Forever Kind of Dream is another Bobtimystic Books
project.

Design, Photography & Editing:
Bob Makela

ISBN-13: 978-0692584804
ISBN-10: 0692584803
Manufactured in the United States of America
First Edition

To order this book or to contact the publisher go to:

www.BobtimysticBooks.com

Suggested retail price: **$13.00**

I'd like to dedicate this book to the love who formed me from the dust of ancient rocks,

to the love who rocked my cradle,

and to the love who rocks my world.

Table of Contents

And now these three remain:
faith, hope and love.
But the greatest of these is love.

~1st Corinthians 13:13

live like the sun, die like a sunset

i will live like the sun;
that golden ball of lemonade dreams.
rising everyday from the east,
triumphantly heralding countless opportunities.
i will rise up to the cerulean sky,
paint the whole world gold,
send rays of smiles across the miles,
warm up hearts and light up souls.
i will make the children forget their nightmares
and dance for joy on the cobbled streets,
give hope to the weary traveler,
and bliss to sowers in far flung lands.
i will beguile the wise laughter of ancient trees
and play on the dunes of silver sand beaches,
splashing this world with God's light
till my last ray lights up the last candle.

i will die like a sunset;
that orange ball of vanilla hopes,
setting royally in the west,
surrounded by the universe i love.
i'll go down with no regrets,
my purpose fulfilled.
my heart will feel no fear, my soul no worries.
and as i descend tranquilly
in a symphony of amber glory,
i'll hold this truth in my heart:
i shall someday rise again
with other glorious suns,
we'll light up the heavens
and never set again.

God is an artist

rembrandt, picasso and leonardo da vinci might be cool
but nothing compares to an artist
who paints the spacious skies a dreamy cerulean blue with
just a word,
paints the galaxies with hues of glorious mystery,
paints you and me with the watercolor of his love,
splashes the world with the spectrum of his grace,
using time as his paper, and the universe as his gallery.

donatello, michelangelo and auguste rodin were great
sculptors
but who is greater than he
who sculpted purple mountain majesties and rolling green
hills
who can stand before him who sculpts men and angels
and made everything beautiful in its time.

angelou, tagore and pablo neruda
might write a thousand and one poems
but who can compare to the poet of poets
who wrote a poem on light and called it the sun
placed it in the first chapter of the sky
and gave it freely, for the world to read every
morning
a poet who rides on the wings of the wind
across golden fields
and gives a poetry reading
that makes the plants dance in glorious delight
to the grace of his quiet words

pacino, de niro and morgan freeman
might win all the oscars
but what star can outshine the star
that left his heavenly throne

and came to earth to play the role of man
a star who transformed every character that crossed his path
walked on ocean waves, calmed the tempest,
healed the sick, rose the dead
broke barriers, leaving his audience in breathless awe
he played the most important role a man will ever play
and gave a performance so powerful that his critics killed him
he won no awards, yet he saved the world.

there have been a million love songs
since the beginning of time
but there is none like the song
that was sung on a dark noon in golgotha
over two thousand years ago by a lowly artist
its lyrics of mercy spilling from an old rugged cross
healing the soul of everyone who listens
john lennon's "imagine" has nothing on the promise of the song,
no chant or melody has ever been more peaceful than it
it's a forever kind of love song that would become
the soundtrack of eternity

God is an artist,
and in you,
he's making a harmonious melody out of the noise,
a miracle out of the dust,
a unique self-portrait of himself,
a masterpiece with his signature of love stamped on it.

geography

so she told the moon
how she had aimed for a man's heart
through his stomach
but instead ended up down south

how easy it had been to pass
geography in high school
but how she flunked badly
when it got down
to the topography of the male heart

what is the way to a man's heart?
did one have to swim through the river of his skin
or walk through the valley of his spleen
was it through the ocean of his eyes
or was it determined by the climate down south
punctuated with hurricanes of primal lust

the moon listened
like it did every night
to the musings of the sons and daughters of the universe
and gave its reply
through the silent still of the night wind;

the way to a man's heart is through his heart,
but first,
you have to find a man with a heart

countless stars in my timeless sky

my life is a memory
filled with thousands of memories.
sparkling above the rest
are the memories i share with you;
they are the sunshine of my days,
the days of my sunshine
the memories that make me who i am
— a part of you.

for we are siamese soul twins
born by different mothers.
separate bodies bonded by one heart;
your heart within my soul,
my soul within your heart.

come away, dearest friend.
let's go to the riverside,
to where the sunset serenades the waters.
let's talk about everything
and laugh about the little things.
reveal all that gladdens
and troubles your spirit
so i could see the world
through your eyes.
for if the sun shines on you,
it shines on me too.
and if the arrow goes through you,
it goes through me too.

let's make this moment count,
let's make it last.
this life is a mysterious journey
we row the boat but God controls the ocean

and if he takes me away from this earth today
or you are gone tomorrow
one thing remains certain;
the moments we create,
these memories we share,
will always be with me
throughout the days of forever.
they are the countless stars in my timeless sky.

tomorrow is yesterday

when I was an old man,
I dreamt of the days of my youth yet to come,
and it made me laugh
that I cried over the wrong things.
now I'm a baby smiling up at my earth guardians,
yet to say my first word,
but my heart is full of wisdom,
my soul remembers the journey.

the house where we grew up

i went to the house where we grew up;
to the rooms that nestled our childhood dreams,
it stood there quiet, still and surreal
like a dream stuck in one scene.

i ran up the stairs we once climbed
and i could hear the sounds.
those treasured sounds of days gone by;
the sound of our laughter,
the sound of our endless chatter,
the sound of our crying
when spanked for our naughtiness,
the sound of the tv tuned in to our favorite cartoon;
tom chasing jerry forever, never catching him,
never giving up either.
i could hear the silence too,
like it used to be when the night had come,
when we quietly lay awake watching the closet,
waiting for a monster to come out and leap on us.

the hallways still bear our scrawling,
our abc's and 123's scribbled all over,
a trace of mom's perfume and dad's shaving powder lingers
in the air
but perhaps it's just my imagination.

let's go back someday
to the house where we grew up.
where headaches and heartaches do not exist.
let's go back and live there forever,
we could play all day long;
play under the sun, play under the stars,
and no one would spank us for our naughtiness.

you could hide my books and toys
knowing i'll always find them and forgive you,

we could be kids forever.
let's go back to the house where we grew up
for it's more than a house,
it's home.

the prayer of wild mountain flowers

I hope one day you walk past a mirror and love your reflection on it. I hope you become your own Picasso and paint your life with love and joy. I hope you laugh till you cry, cry till you laugh, dance till you lose yourself. I hope your life becomes a golden boulevard of days stretching into a colorful forever. I hope you find a lover who injects the ecstasy of a thousand laughing oceans into your heart, as you do the same. I hope you stand bravely for everything you believe in. I hope you do bad things and yet remain good. I hope you write that story you've always wanted to write, and you live a life that'll be an inspiring story to all who read your footprints. I hope when the sky opens and takes you in that you waltz merrily through the galaxies...

watermelon dawn

on our first night together
we stayed awake till 3am
talking about God, outer space and poetry.
and as the words flowed from your lips,
i finally realized where the sun goes
after it sets in the evening;
it goes to your heart.
your heart is the resting place
of love's eternal sun.

my favorite picture of you

my favorite picture of you is yet to be taken.
it's a window side portrait of you at eighty;
your face a happy marriage of laugh lines and wisdom,
your body a weathered temple
I still come to worship in.

my favorite picture of you is yet to be taken.
it's a window side portrait of you at eighty;
your hair has become the color of ocean foam,
your skin seasoned by sun and sand.
it's nothing like the selfies of your youth
but never in eight decades have you looked more beautiful.

let's run away

take my hands and let's run away,
let's run to the edge of the world.
we'll leave ordinary behind
and take only things legends and myths are made of
we'll go to lengths only lions go, rise to heights
only eagles see
view the ocean through the eyes of a dolphin
and hear the soul of the universe
in the crashing waves of the pacific at midnight.

we'll learn we are one with the trees in the Amazon
and that the kangaroos in the plains of Australia are
our long lost brothers
we'll discover the earth was our first mother
and our father isn't in the sky
but in every one of us.
we'll find angels in the dark street alleys of Haiti
and discover we are the angels we found.

we'll crash a traditional wedding in Thailand
and dance with the locals
getting drunk on life
as stars light up the Bangkok sky
we'll get married ourselves on Christmas day
in an old church in Buenos Aires
and honeymoon in a new house in Nairobi
filled with old wine and old books

let's run away
we've been standing in the same spot for so long
seeing the same view from the window for ages.
let's run away to the edge of the world
and come back home with new eyes.

soar

i've packed up a bag filled with my past
heartaches and things that did not last
i'll mail it to the bottom of the ocean
free my heart from every negative emotion.

i'll ride to the top and never look back
focus on the light and never on the dark
up above is a sky yearning for me to soar through it
a world waiting for a world-changing feat

and as the world gradually steps aside
while i rise to the heights irrespective of the tide
i'll hold my guard against the wind's roar
take a leap of faith and soar.

here's to the girls whose fathers broke their hearts before any boy could

he was meant to be your first dream
but he became your first nightmare
his soul was a stranger to you
and now you've become a stranger to yours
his memory is a scar atop your heart
a pain from all your yesterdays
but fair one, just as a tree is not identified with the leaves
it shed in stormy february,
you are not the scars from a wilted past.
you are a sky born anew every morning
a love blooming in the present
so make art from the beating of your heart
write a new story
and paint forgiveness over the wrinkled dawn
walk strong on your path
and even when the memories of yesterday come your way
like a hurricane
stand your ground,
it shall pass
for you are no longer held by the shackles of days bygone.
you are free
you are an independent country
and your anthem is peace

of a pearl who thought she was mud

you are the whole expanse of the glorious night sky;
magnificent by nature, majestic to behold,
but all your dazzling stars have been hidden
by clouds of insecurity

you are God's love song to the world
the greatest ballad ever, a melody made of stardust
but you've turned down your volume
and the world can't hear your lyrics

you are a pearl,
everything bright, brilliant, and beautiful
but you're hidden within an oyster shell of fears
lost in a monstrous sea of self-doubt

you are the center of God's most central thoughts,
the most vivid dream of the universe,
a miracle created to create miracles,
the seed of a great oak tree
waiting to bloom into a forest

so bloom Darling
burst out from the oyster shell of fears
that is too small to contain your big pearl of dreams
break away from clouds of insecurity
that have nothing on your array of stars of possibility
turn up the volume of your life's music
and let the world dance to the rhythm
of a life well-lived.

awesome huesome

my true colors were buzzing in me
sapient shades of surrealistic splendor
but i hid from the magnificence of it all
under a mask of blind blandness.

then you came my way messenger of love
and lifted me on your wings to the morning sun
till its rays permeated the core of my being,
all the scales of lies melting under the heat of truth

and i beheld the crimson glory of my spirit
i tasted the psychedelic purple of my soul
i felt the smoky topaz of my body

see me now
maskless, fearless, alive
disco ball of love spiraling wild through the galaxies
my true colors freely singing the song
the creator taught them ages ago
long before the serpent deceived eve.

masterpiece

sing a song of my love
it's the joyful chorus of a million singing angels,
melody reaching earth through starlight
it's the unshackled harmony of the ocean waves
passionately kissing the shore from dawn to dusk
it's a symphony orchestra
playing in tune to my heartbeat

write a book of my love
it's a never-ending story of a never-ending love
an ancient parable on forgiveness
it's an anthology of poems written
on the wings of doves
it's a series of love letters with unfaded words
found in the ruins of Solomon's temple

paint a picture of my love
it's the timeless picture of a smiling sun
it's the dance of the wind through a rose garden
it's the quiet joy of a blooming pomegranate orchard
it's the image of two swans flying across
a watermelon sky

come all ye singers, writers, artists
and fellow adventurers on this narrow path
come let's make blissful art
out of love.
for everything done in love, with love
and for love, is a masterpiece.

black unicorn

you say you are weird.
you think you are nothing.
but i think it's weird
you don't see the something
within this "nothing."

you show me your scars.
you tell me your past is real.
but this is the right time
to let go of the past
and its scars,
and look into the now
and its stars.

you tell me you're a freak.
you feel awkward in your own skin.
but i think you are beautifully different,
like a black unicorn
in a sea of white horses.

you want to lock yourself inside forever.
hide in the shadow of long kept fears.
but i want to run with you
through the crowded streets,
shout to the whole world
how amazing you are.

it does not matter
what illusions you have about yourself,
or what box
the world has labeled you in.
to me, you are love's first child.
the most enthralling thing in the universe.

art of hearts

let's be an art of hearts, forever...

the world is full of love poems
but i don't want to read another.
i want us to be the poem others read
i want my thoughts to be a sonnet to you
my words to be a ballad of our love
my actions to be an ode to us
every little thing we do
rhyming with the poetry
of dancing roses in the valley

the world is full of love stories
but i don't want to read another.
i want us to become one.
let us be that fairy tale
that parents would read to their kids
generations from now.
let's become the book on the shelf
that the library never discards.
a story that would sail on the wings of time
and become one with the wind
engraved forever in the memory of the universe

the world is full of love songs
but i don't want to listen to another.
i want us to become one.
i want your name to be the song
i sing in the shower at dawn,
i want your laughter
to be the soundtrack of my days,
i want to slow dance to the silence of the words
you say with your eyes,

i want the world to put its ear to my chest
and hear your heart beating within mine.
let's be art
let's be the eternal poem
the rainbow reads to the earth after a storm
let's be the immortal story
the moon tells the stars every night
let's be that timeless love song
the sky sings to the ocean whenever she's sad
let's be an art of hearts, forever...
you

<u>bubblysunnylovejoymiracle</u>

ever since I met you, my vocabulary has expanded.
I tell my friends of all the Superfantasticoolawesome
you say and write poems on all the
Beauticharmintelligentkind
things you do.
autocorrect keeps trying to correct me,
Google keeps saying those words don't exist
but I think God understands me
when I pray and thank him for
the Bubblysunnylovejoymiracle
that you are.

the reality of you

they say a rose in bloom
is the most beautiful thing ever
but i guess they've never seen your smile.

they rave about how a walk
through the great wall of china
is the most exciting thing ever
but i think they've never walked through
a winding path with you.

they talk about the wonders of the world
they travel faraway to see
the splendors of the universe
but i look into your eyes and see it all in your soul

Men have dreamt dreams
written fairy tales
spun tales and fantasies
but no dream
no fairy tale
no grandeur tale
or fantasy
compares
to the reality of you

where God lives

He could have chosen the amber shores or
the crimson skies
or perhaps the deepest part of the deepest ocean
He could have picked the biggest cathedral in rome
or a lowly temple in budapest
a faraway planet could have been His choice to make,
or a shooting star that falls once in ten thousand years
He had countless choices,
a billion places He could have made His dwelling place
instead He chose my heart
and made it His home.

iris

what if
there are no mirrors
no cameras
no selfies
and the only way
to know what you look like
is to look at another
and know your perception of them
is your very reflection.

universe

what is the ocean but liquid sky

what are days but brighter nights

what are diamonds but the memory of ancient laughter

what is forever but a never-ending now

who am I but another you

oaks by the river

grow in love with me
grow crazy with me
grow wild with me
grow in beauty with me
grow in grace with me
grow in wisdom with me
grow in spirit with me
grow old with me

finding you

finding you
was like discovering
the love child of a unicorn and dragon,
hidden in the secret chamber of a long-lost ship,
sailing on a tempest-ridden enchanted sea,
off the coast of a long-deserted island.

poets of distant planets

i want to meet the poets of distant planets;
see what kind of fire burns in their bones,
taste the cosmos through alien words,
and get drenched in the metaphors of outer space.

i want to meet the poets of distant planets;
find out if they've ever knitted poems comprised only
of loose strands of sadness,
or painted ballads of overflowing joy,
discover if their souls have ever ached deeply for
another soul,
or if love is just a human illness?

dying to stay alive

Love;
a near-death experience,
an out-of-the-body occurrence,
I fall with the rain from roaring skies
and splash into oneness with the sea.
spectators huddled in raincoats on the shore
label me a dead man,
but never have I felt more alive.

made in China

i'm in a shop trying to look for something that's not
MADE IN CHINA
but everywhere i turn i find something that's
MADE IN CHINA
from toothpaste to the wig on the attendant's head, it's all
MADE IN CHINA
i stomp out and head to the restaurant to eat something that's not
MADE IN CHINA
for all i need is fufu and soup but all they have is food that's
MADE IN CHINA
i stomp right out and get splashed all over by a car that's
MADE IN CHINA
i head home and change into clothes that unsurprisingly were
MADE IN CHINA
and as i sit in front of a computer that was (you guessed right)
MADE IN CHINA
i conclude that God created heaven and earth and every other thing was
MADE IN CHINA.

orgasm

the whole universe
is an orgasm of God's love,
and when we do things with passion,
with the innate love of the spirit,
we have an orgasm within an orgasm.
anything lower than that
is just bad sex.

<u>sparkle</u>

be thankful for monday mornings as you are for
friday evenings,
dance even more in july than you did in
december,
let love become the rhythm of your life
so that every meal becomes a communion
every journey a pilgrimage

forgive the stars on nights when they don't shine
just as they forgive you on nights
when they shine and you don't appreciate 'em.
some days would taste as sour as lemons
but that's just what you need for your lemonade.
some days would taste as sweet as
watermelons,
go ahead and make your watermelon wine.
your tears are silver, your smiles are gold
don't be ashamed of a table that has both,

the magic you've been seeking is inside
your actions would be the wand,
this grand universe your stage.
let the show begin.
sparkle!

the long road to love

the world is an ocean of hearts;
billions of hearts filled with different desires,
but rising above the rest is the desire for love,
the hunger for companionship.

and it has always been with us,
this quest for love,
from our days of infancy,
when our tiny frames sought after
the comforting warmth of our parents' arms,
for the soothing sound of a lullaby
and a touch to assure us we are loved.

as we grow older, it never changes
for we seek the same things we sought as a child
in a different way;
the comforting arms of a soulmate,
the soothing music of a lover's voice,
and a touch to assure us we are loved.

amidst this all,
the hole in our souls cry out
and we continue our quest for a higher kind of love,
for a creator in whom we find our purpose
while discovering a divine kind of love.

and as we travel through life,
we might occasionally take the wrong path
but we must learn to forgive ourselves and everyone
and retrace our steps back to the long road to love
for only when we discover
that our journey on earth is a lesson in love
and our universal purpose for existing is love,
shall we begin to live.
and all we can do while we wait for eternity
is to love always, love truly and love unconditionally.

footprints on the waters (the sea walker)

i took the same journey you currently take,
i took it a long time ago.
my journey was more stormy than yours,
strong winds and waves hitting from every angle,
but above the chaos i stood,
nature's elements bowing to me,
i walked through the storm
leaving my footprints on the waters.

now as you walk through this temporary storm,
remember my promise to you:
i'll never leave nor forsake you,
remember, as i am so are you.
so fear not the raging wind, let it fear you instead.
worry not about the waves, for you are higher than them.
i'm with you, in you, behind you, before you, i'm everywhere.
i'll walk with you through the storm
till you get to the still waters.
i'll cleave to you in love,
giving you something to hold on to
in a world that spins crazily around.

he walks among us

i've walked through the streets of the world;
from the quiet lanes of iceland
to the war-torn roads of syria,
i've waded through the markets of bombay
and sat on the beaches of mombassa.
the sun has dried out my skin,
the sole of my feet blistered by rocks.
my clothes threadbare and thin,
my hair long and unkept.
some of the sons of men
have been kind.
they've offered me a helping hand
filled with
food, clothing, warmth and love.
others shut the door on my face
and spit on the sand.
they scrunch up their noses
and ignore me.
they've prayed all their lives
to see God.
little do they know
they've just walked past him.

through the eyes of God(Love)

i sat on the cradle of time
and looked through the pages of ages
my mind sailing through the purest light
my heart looking at the world
through the eyes of God(Love)

those eyes that saw
a whole nation in a barren couple
and
a great leader in a runaway prince
eyes that saw
a heroine of faith in a prostitute
and
a powerful king in a shepherd boy

eyes made up of
an iris of compassion
lens of truth
and a retina of grace
looking beyond the skin
into the innermost cloves of the heart,
seeing the deepest of the deepest thoughts
beholding the hidden core
of the human soul

i sat on the cradle of time
and looked at the world
through the eyes of God(Love)
and i learned
that the only thing worth viewing is the invisible

Christmas angels

they will drop softly from the sky,
amidst the dazzling white
of countless snowflakes;
beautiful angels bearing gifts
wrapped with God's love.
they will mingle with the crowd,
cleverly disguised as humans.
they will hang out in the parks,
the streets and the churches,
seeking whom to bless.
and men will hurriedly walk past the angels,
ignoring them in their futile search
for a non-existent santa claus.

postcards from heaven

Let the doors of heaven be opened
and millions of doves
showered upon the earth,
flying down with sunshine on their feathers,
millions of flapping wings
turning wind into music.
let them cover the land,
every rooftop, treetop and hilltop
feathery postcards from the skies,
cooing a message of peace,
and when the world opens its window
to behold this avian splendor,
may they fall in love with God again.

amina is not dead

dearest amina, i heard you knock on my door
and call out my name
while it was raining last night.
i ran down the stairs
and opened the door but you were gone.
i looked for you under the rain,
searched for you on the dark streets
but i didn't find you
though i knew you were hiding,
merging with the shadows
watching me
and laughing at your silly joke.

they say you are dead,
they claim you got knocked down by a truck
but i think they are crazy,
for how can life itself die?
so i smiled throughout the duration of your "wake,"
i laughed out loud during your "funeral"
for that couldn't be you in the coffin,
no, it was just another girl who looked like you.
you are such a joker and you've played the biggest joke
on us.
i'm sure you finally ran away to paris like you always dreamt
you will
but why didn't you take me along?
they say i'm in denial, they think i'm mad
but they don't know you as much as i do;
you are life, you are the ocean.
life never dies and the ocean is forever.

dearest amina, it's six months since you've been gone
and i've been indoors all this while.
all that's left are the pictures and the memories

but you are more than a picture, more than a memory
i no longer jog in the morning or hang out in the park
for what if i go out and you come back and find
no one home.
the days are cold and the hours are lonely but
i sit here waiting

for i'm sure you'll be back soon.
you'll knock on the door and call out my name,
i'll run down the stairs and open the door
and this time you'll be standing there
with the wind in your hair and the sun in your eyes,
i'll run into your arms and never ever let go.

<u>songs of our lives</u>

aren't songs just memories set to music?

I hear some songs and I remember my childhood,
running barefoot through narrow streets
and sailing the wind,
with the voice of my mother
on my back like angel wings.

I hear some songs and I remember my teenage years;
the angst, the acne, peer pressure and society's poison
all bottled up under my skin.

I hear some songs
and the door to my heart is opened,
to long-forgotten corners
where five thousand memories live,
days and nights spent living under God's sky.

I hear some songs
and I remember you,
wearing my t-shirt
and snuggled up in my arms,
whispering you'll stay with me forever
but forgetting to mention your forever had an expiry date.

don't forget to remember me

do you remember
falling asleep outside,
beneath a willow tree,
billions of stars in the dusky sky
forming a glittering blanket
above you

do you remember
awakening to the cocks' crow,
a thousand birds singing out the tune of the dawn
in the dew-touched meadow,
your mellifluous laughter tinkling
away the traces of night

do you still cry at the sight of a sunset,
your heart touched by a beauty
that does not compare to yours

do you smile
when you remember my singing,
how your ears begged for mercy
from my out-of-tune drone.

does the fragrance of these memories
still linger on
or have they been lost
in the inane whirl
of the fast cars and skyscrapers
of the city?

the lilies you planted
are now in full bloom,
growing wildly and encompassing the whole place
like your love did to my heart.

i ponder no more
on your decision to leave,
for your high heels
and fancy dresses were meant for the city
not the
untamed countryside

but for how long
would your high heels and the high life
control your heart,
my dearest dear ?

when the city lights
dazzle you no more,
when the high life makes you low,
and you long for the simple life,
let your heart guide you home
and i'll still be here,
tending to the wild lilies you left behind.

but in the meantime,
don't forget the tangerine sunset,
remember the ocean waves
hitting the rocky shore,
recall the morning dew on your skin,
recollect the long walks,
remember chuks, our puppy,
remember my voice in your ears,
and wherever you are,
my morning rose,
don't forget to remember me.

reality is but a dream (la réalité n'est qu'un rêve)

on that day
you'll realize
there is more to this journey
than what you see.
the physical will fade away
like the morning mist.
your spirit would rise,
shining brighter than the afternoon sun.

vous allez enfin comprendre
le langage de la pluie
et la musique des étoiles.
vous verrez Dieu,
il ne sera pas un étranger.

sing the songs
you were born to sing.
write the books
you were born to write.
smile under the sun
that shines just for you.

gba egwu di n'obi gi
chefu ihe echiche.
ofu ndu bu nke gi.
dance as if it's your last dance
on your last day on earth.

kiss the one you love
with the passion
of a thousand thundering waterfalls,
taste their soul on your lips.
lie in their arms forever.

love beyond words.
perdonar y te perdonará
la vida es una lección sobre el amor.
buscar lo eterno.
the seasons will fade away,
the reason will stay.
reality is but a dream.

the reasons behind the reasons (for nick vujicic)

the reason behind the reasons
without arms, you touched my soul
without legs, you walked into my heart
inspiring me to look beyond what i see
for there are lot of mysteries in this world
grey areas we don't understand
but someday when heaven kisses the earth
and the eternal light dispels the shadows
we'll understand the reason behind the reasons
but for now i hang on to your message:
why complain that the night has come
when you can rejoice that the stars are here.

angels and superheroes

we may not have wings
but with love we can lift everyone
who is broken and helpless.

golden robes may not be ours
but with our words and actions
we can outshine the finest gold.

we may not have magical swords
to fight the villains,
but within us
is an ocean of light and goodness
that can overcome
the desert of darkness and evil
that tries to encroach the world.

we may not have the power
to make the sun shine always
but when the day goes dim
and the hope of men wavers,
we can awaken the world
with the light in our spirit.

we may not have magical powers
and we may not be angels and superheroes,
but we could be everything
angels and superheroes should be

<u>home</u>

i climbed the hill to find it;
if it wasn't home,
it must be on the hill, i thought,
but it wasn't there.

i climbed the mountain to find it;
if it wasn't home or on the hill,
it must be on the mountain, i thought,
but it wasn't there.

i swam across the river to find it;
if it wasn't home, on the hill or the mountain,
it must be in the river, i thought,
but it wasn't there.

my feet aching,
heart bruised and spirit crushed,
i swam back the river, crossed the mountain,
got down the hill
and headed back home.

i got home
as the last of the midnight candles flickered out.
and there it was
lighting up the atmosphere
with the dazzle of a supernova.

the treasure i had traveled all over to find
had been home all this while
just waiting for me
to open the eyes of my heart.

dream

the rain might fall all day
and hide away the sun's ray
the world might look bleak
and the clock might refuse to tick
still i'll dream

the opposition might be strong
and the storm may seem so long
the world might turn its back on me
and grey may be all i see
still my dreams will stand firm.

the world may be a big riddle
but even if life is the eye of a needle
and my dreams a camel
my dreams will walk on through
for they are meant to come true

<u>life</u>

alas, isn't life a journey
of learning what we already know,
of taking new trips to places we've already been,
of finding and falling in love with people
we've actually loved beyond this time and clime,
of getting to heaven and finding out it's a place on earth

Gemini

you are both the sanguine face of the sun and the ru-
minative spirit of the moon,
and I am the open arms of the sky longing to hold you
in brightest morn and sombre dusk.

you are equal parts an eternal child and an immortal
old soul,
teaching me wisdom through foolish little acts of love.

you are water and wine.
winter, spring, summer and autumn all rolled in one.
the energy of a new beginning and the ease of the
seventh day of rest.
you are a tree fluent in the language of wildflowers.

now you lure me in with the magic flute of your words
into the enchanted landscape of your being
and I'll stay with you
surfing the waves of your years
down the ocean of time.

BeautifulCrazyWildLoveBeing

you who has fireflies serenading your feet
with an ancient tune of love
when you walk through the grassy paths at night

you who has shooting stars
falling down from outer space
so they could make a wish on you

you who when asleep
has the moon leaving its sky
and coming to your window
to get a closer view of you

you whose immortal soul
the morning sun longs, craves
and dreams to shine like

you who has trees, from gardens in Karachi
to orchards in Santorini,
singing a song of your beauty
in flower verses and fruit choruses

you BeautifulCrazyWildLoveBeing
running free through the streets of the earth
baptizing eyes with your grace

you, you are love and you are loved.

forgive me for the parts of you i'm yet to kiss

i used to think there was only one part of
the body meant for kisses,
but on your body I discovered a thousand places.

you were born naked so I could clothe you with kisses,
my lips were made to adorn every inch of
the landscape of your skin.

kisses on places you'll never want your mother
to read about,
sinful actions too holy for confession.

and when we finally merge into one
my body memorizing every part of yours
i discover there are ways to visit heaven without dying.

sanctuary

I once saw a picture of a temple
with a steeple so high it kissed the sky.
I've been inside cathedrals
made of stained glass, pine and seasoned mahogany.
I've read of Solomon's temple;
how it was made of pure gold, olive wood
and cedars from lebanon.
but beloved, even the glorious combination
of all these temples
does not compare to how sacred and beautiful
the temple of your body is,
how every fiber of you
reverberates with light.

I rise higher to the sight of you
at the break of dawn
and thrust deeper to the feel of you
at the edge of dusk.
every moment with you is a prayer,
my heart forever on its knees with gratitude.
you lay your hands on me
and lead me through a path of grace
to the doorstep of your soul,
to the threshold of the origin of love
where my imperfections are forgiven one kiss at a time.
I pull closer to you
and move in sync to the oceans roaring inside of you,
faster, harder, deeper.
every stroke taking me closer to heaven,
and nearer to nirvana,
as I gradually become one with the sky.

the mad bard

you make me
never want to wear underwear again
but strut through crowded streets
and lonely hallways,
wearing nothing but the scent of you
underneath my trousers.

sunset walks and endless tangerine moments

we walk hand-in-hand through the tranquil woods,
dry leaves and twigs crunching softly beneath our feet.
the last rays of the orange sunset get caught in your hair,
as birds fly home through the sunset sky.

we talk about childhood dreams and grown-up hopes.
Promises our hearts have kept,
secrets only our souls know.
from a distance, the ocean waves roar with joy.
in the roar we hear an eternal voice;
a voice of passion, the voice of God.

we write our name on the bark of an apple tree
like the way we write it in our hearts everyday.
and in this moment, we are infinite.
two souls taking one journey.

lying by the banks of a brook
we watch as the woods come aglow with
stars and fireflies.
and as the sun makes its final descent
and the moon arises from the clouds,
i lean over and give you a kiss
as passionate as the september sun,
a kiss as endless as forever.

making memories

time dances freely
to the tranquil ballet of God's grace
seconds spinning swiftly
o'er the ever-changing clime of our lives
today's moment becomes tomorrow's memory
tomorrow's memory, just another chapter
in the book of forever

so stay with me
and let's make these moments
become memories
that the seasons cannot erase
from long sunny days
spent in the sequestered
swings of our secret garden,
eating wild fruits and tasting sunlight
to long cold nights
spent making love,
all night long, by the fireplace
my tongue serenading your coffee skin

let's spend the days of our youth
living our dreams, forgiving our flaws,
sharing the love
that has been shed abroad in our hearts
till we grow old
and leave this side of eternity
let's live each moment so beautifully well
that on the day the angels play our lives before us
we'll gladly tell them
to press the replay button
over and over again.

nkem

nkem, we'll become dust,
like we did before,
like we will again,
but somewhere in between the memories of our
future past and dreams yet to be born,
I'll find you.
you'll return to me in different
skin shades and genders
but your eyes would remain the same.

in new worlds with divergent tongues and
brand new names,
I'll find you nkem.
you won't be a stranger.
my eyes would remember yours.

eternal childhood

are you my childhood?
you reek of cartoon-fueled Saturday mornings,
swings that made me kiss the sky,
glorious days when my happy little feet
ran through a kaleidoscope of colors.
I remember you.
I miss you.
stay forever this time.

a lifetime with you

from the dawn of our first kiss
to the dusk of our last breath,
all that i dream of
is a lifetime with you.

from the cry of our first baby
to the smile of our last grandchild,
all that i pray for
is a lifetime with you.

a lifetime
basking
in the glory of your smile
and drinking
from the spring of your grace.

a lifetime standing by your side
through the days
when life feels like a walk through a wildflower garden
to the days
when life seems
like a forest of storms.

a lifetime in your arms,
in your heart,
in your soul.

from our last walk on earth
to our first walk in heaven.
all that i see
is a lifetime with you.

eclipse of the heart

oh brother,
what happened to the light
that shined so brightly in your heart?
from whence does this menacing shadow come?
the world has been cruel to you
and your heart has retreated under the darkness.

oh brother,
what happened to the love
you gave so freely to everyone?
why this sudden eclipse of the heart?
the warm spring that once overflowed
now lays cold and barren.

oh brother,
remember your childhood dreams,
the promises of yesterday.
remember the miracle of a sunrise,
and don't forget every new day is a treasure field,
waiting for you to explore
so you could discover grace for every moment.

oh brother,
when you can stand no more,
and your heart refuses to sparkle,
just reach into my heart
for i have enough light to carry the two of us
and together, step by step, one day at a time
we will dispel the shadow from your heart.

__rudy__

rudy on my mind
childhood friends with
a mischievous streak
laughing and running through narrow streets
with a naughty prank up our sleeves.

rudy on my mind
teenage buddies with hearts broken a dozen times
and breath taken away a hundred times
by those angels in human form.

rudy on my mind
the twenties have come.
rebels with a cause,
living under a troubled sky
yet waiting for our dreams to come true.

rudy on my mind
the thirties are here
fathers we've become
though we never did grow up
children becoming fathers to children.

time keeps flying by
the universe keeps breathing
seconds turning into minutes,
minutes into hours, hours into days,
days into years...

rudy on my mind
golden oldies we've become
bones starting to creak
the once-sturdy tree starts to shed its leaves.

rudy on my mind
the sun has set in the east
my red rose contrasting to the gray pallor of your grave.

rudy on my mind
an eternal friend
memories running on and on in my head
like a forever kind of dream.

heaven's child

i will see you the moment
i step through the pearl gates of heaven.
for amidst thousands of angels
you stand out.
In your heart i'll find God's love
in your face his grace.
you'll hold my hand
and walk with me through the streets of heaven,
teaching me new songs of joy
and showing me how the angels dance.
old tears and fears will be forgotten
as love and peace completely surround us.
and on those golden streets,
where tigers joyfully play with lambs,
and the laughter of happy children resounds forever,
i will look down the road
and see God smiling at me.

the ecstasy of love

being of light
do you remember the streets of gold?
do you recall running free with stars, tame lions and
angels on the palms of God?
do you get the blues, a longing for
a place that is not here?
the camera not even capturing what you feel.
be still.
we are only the adopted children of mother earth.
you are made from a light that
scientists cannot comprehend.
galaxies in the farthest plains of the universe
know your name.
breathe.
your soul longs for Paradise,
seeking for it in absurd places,
getting lost in dark spaces.
but only when we lose ourselves to
the ecstasy of love,
do we find ourselves, alive with joy,
closer and closer to heaven.

endless

i don't want this
to be like the story of romeo and juliet
with its tragical ending,
or the tale of prince charming and cinderella
with its happy ending.
i want this to have no ending.

moments flowing into years,
years cascading into infinity,
time fading away...

your soul and mine,
forever watering our flowers of love
with showers of faith
in a garden of hope.

your poem

i am the poet
you are the poem
i hold the pen
and you are the words i write
flowing from deep within me
making my every move
an expression of love

you are the sky
and i'm the sun
cleaving to you with love
through stormy mornings and calm noons
serenading you as the seasons roll into forever

you are the thought that awakens my smile
the smile that arouses my laughter
the laughter that kindles my joy
the joy that illuminates my life
my life which i live for you

someday we'll die
and wildflowers will grow on our graves
these moments will become stardust
as we pass from this dream to divine reality
but every time my story is told
your name will be celebrated
for you are my 'once upon a time'
and my 'happily ever after'
every song i sing is yours
every little poem i write is for you.

Ifeanyi Ogbo lives in Nigeria.

This is his first book of poetry.

www.ingramcontent.com/pod-product-compliance
Lightning Source LLC
LaVergne TN
LVHW041235080426
835508LV00011B/1214